Max Fox and His Sax

By Carmel Reilly

The fans are here for Max.

Max has a sax.

Max hops up.

He jabs at the sax.

No! The sax is bad!

The fans are mad.

Max taps at the sax
and tips it.

"I can fix the sax," said Yak.

Max begs the fans
not to quit.

Rox taps.

Zac zigs and zags.

Max raps and hums.

Yak gets the sax to Max.

The fans get up
and hop and bop.

CHECKING FOR MEANING

1. Why were the fans mad? *(Literal)*

2. Who was able to fix the sax? *(Literal)*

3. Why did the fans hop and bop when Max Fox played his sax? *(Inferential)*

EXTENDING VOCABULARY

fix	What does it mean to *fix* something? Is there more than one meaning for this word? If you take away the *f* and put another letter at the start, what other words can you make that rhyme with *fix*?
quit	What does it mean to *quit*? Why would the fans *quit* at The Hut?
zigs and zags	What do these words mean in the text? How would Zac *zig and zag?*

MOVING BEYOND THE TEXT

1. What is the name of a band that you like? Why do you like them?

2. What musical instruments are often played in a band?

3. How is a saxophone played?

4. Have you ever been to a concert where a band played? Did you enjoy it? Why?

SPEED SOUNDS

Xx	Yy	Zz		
Kk	Ll	Vv	Qq	Ww
Dd	Jj	Oo	Gg	Uu
Cc	Bb	Rr	Ee	Ff	Hh	Nn
Mm	Ss	Aa	Pp	Ii	Tt

PRACTICE WORDS

sax

Max

fix

Rox

Yak

Zac

zigs

zags

Fix

Yes